WOMEN IN STEM
ROSALIND FRANKLIN
DNA TRAILBLAZER

by Clara MacCarald

pogo

Ideas for Parents and Teachers

Pogo Books let children practice reading informational text while introducing them to nonfiction features such as headings, labels, sidebars, maps, and diagrams, as well as a table of contents, glossary, and index.

Carefully leveled text with a strong photo match offers early fluent readers the support they need to succeed.

Before Reading

- "Walk" through the book and point out the various nonfiction features. Ask the student what purpose each feature serves.
- Look at the glossary together. Read and discuss the words.

Read the Book

- Have the child read the book independently.
- Invite him or her to list questions that arise from reading.

After Reading

- Discuss the child's questions. Talk about how he or she might find answers to those questions.
- Prompt the child to think more. Ask: Did you know about Rosalind Franklin before reading this book? What more would you like to learn about her life and work with DNA?

Pogo Books are published by Jump!
5357 Penn Avenue South
Minneapolis, MN 55419
www.jumplibrary.com

Library of Congress Cataloging-in-Publication Data

Names: MacCarald, Clara, 1979- author.
Title: Rosalind Franklin: DNA trailblazer / by Clara MacCarald.
Description: Minneapolis, MN: Jump!, Inc., [2024]
Series: Women in STEM | Includes index.
Audience: Ages 7-10
Identifiers: LCCN 2023030091 (print)
LCCN 2023030092 (ebook)
ISBN 9798889967101 (hardcover)
ISBN 9798889967118 (paperback)
ISBN 9798889967125 (ebook)
Subjects: LCSH: Franklin, Rosalind, 1920-1958–Juvenile literature. | Women molecular biologists–Juvenile literature. | DNA–Juvenile literature.
Classification: LCC QP26.F68 M32 2024 (print)
LCC QP26.F68 (ebook)
DDC 572.8082–dc23/eng/20230712
LC record available at https://lccn.loc.gov/2023030091
LC ebook record available at https://lccn.loc.gov/2023030092

Editor: Katie Chanez
Designer: Emma Almgren-Bersie

Photo Credits: Photo 12/Alamy, cover (foreground); BeholdingEye/iStock, cover (DNA); Shutterstock, cover (background), 14-15 (background); agefotostock/Alamy, 1; ithinksky/iStock, 3; MattL_Images/Shutterstock, 4 (left); Science Source, 4 (right); Van de Wiel Photography/Shutterstock, 5; lusia83/Shutterstock, 6; ClassicStock/Alamy, 6-7; National Physical Laboratory/Crown Copyright/Science Source, 8-9; nakaridore/Shutterstock, 10; Science History Images/Alamy, 11, 14 (foreground); An.B/Shutterstock, 12; Henry Grant Collection/Museum of London, 12-13; anusorn nakdee/iStock, 16-17; cynoclub/Shutterstock, 18 (left); photomaster/Shutterstock, 18 (right); janiecbros/iStock, 19; VITTORIO LUZZATI/Science Source, 20-21; Cimmerian/iStock, 23.

Printed in the United States of America at Corporate Graphics in North Mankato, Minnesota.

TABLE OF CONTENTS

CHAPTER 1

STUDYING COAL

Have you heard of **DNA**? Do you know what it looks like? Rosalind Franklin helped scientists learn more about it. But for many years, few people knew about her.

DNA

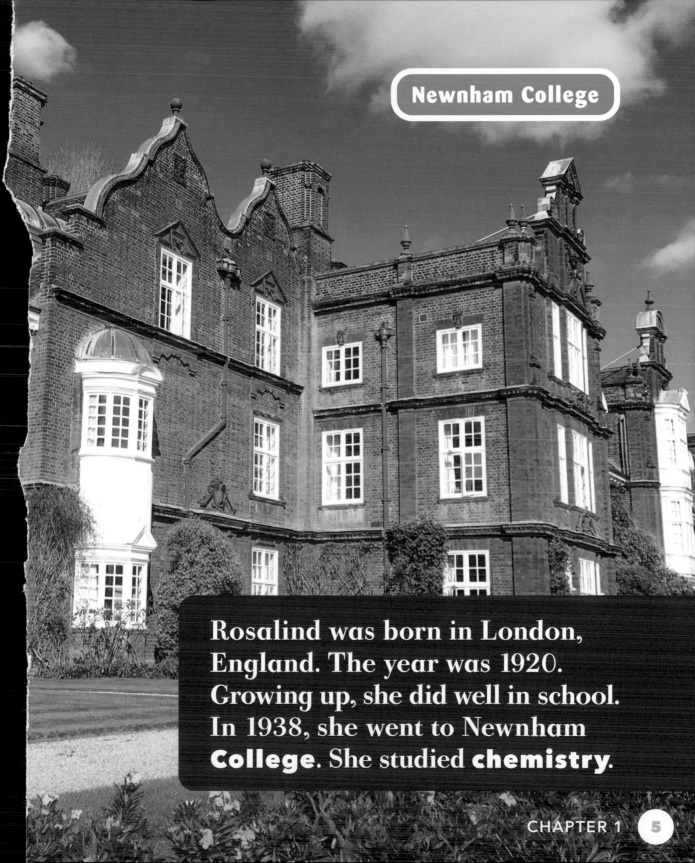

Newnham College

Rosalind was born in London, England. The year was 1920. Growing up, she did well in school. In 1938, she went to Newnham **College**. She studied **chemistry**.

World War II began in 1939. Many scientists helped the war effort. Rosalind was one. After college, she looked at coal. She studied its **structure**. Why? It affects how coal burns. Her work helped people burn coal more **efficiently**. This helped the war effort. How? Coal powered factories. Some made materials for the war.

DID YOU KNOW?

Rosalind's research was used to make gas masks. They were worn during the war. They helped **filter** poisons in the air. They made air safer to breathe.

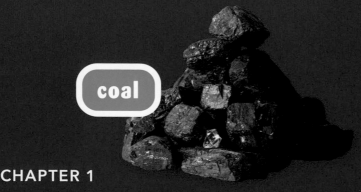

coal

factory

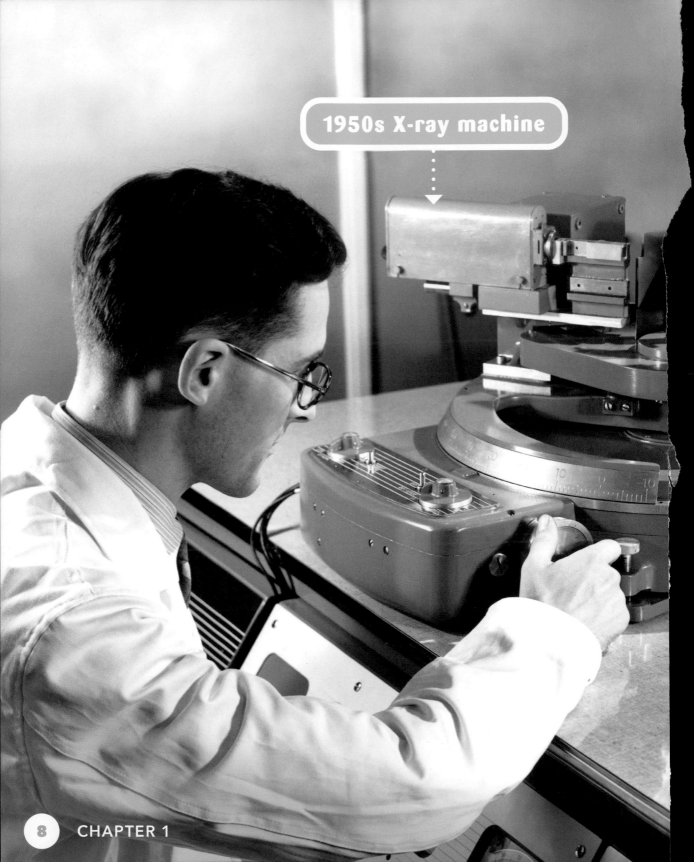

1950s X-ray machine

The war ended in 1945. Rosalind moved to France. She studied **molecules**. She looked at their structure.

She sent **X-rays** into **carbon**. The X-rays bounced off. They made patterns. She took pictures of the patterns. Then, she used math. She figured out what the molecules look like.

She loved the French lab she worked in. The scientists were friendly. Women were welcome.

CHAPTER 2

· ·

STUDYING DNA

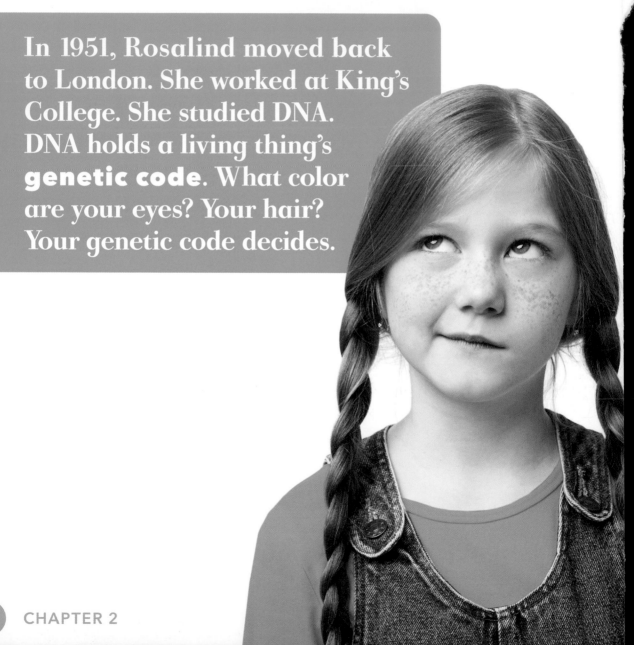

In 1951, Rosalind moved back to London. She worked at King's College. She studied DNA. DNA holds a living thing's **genetic code**. What color are your eyes? Your hair? Your genetic code decides.

Maurice Wilkins

Female scientists at King's College were not treated the same as males. Maurice Wilkins led the lab. He and Rosalind did not get along.

She continued her work anyway. She sent X-rays into DNA. She measured the patterns. The patterns were often unclear. She thought DNA was shaped like a **helix**. But she was not sure.

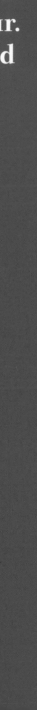

helix

Rosalind's photo of DNA

James Watson and Francis Crick also studied DNA. Maurice showed them Rosalind's pictures. The men also found some of her math.

Rosalind's work allowed the men to make a big discovery. They figured out Rosalind was on the right track. DNA is a double helix.

DID YOU KNOW?

Rosalind also studied viruses. Viruses are tiny. They can make people sick.

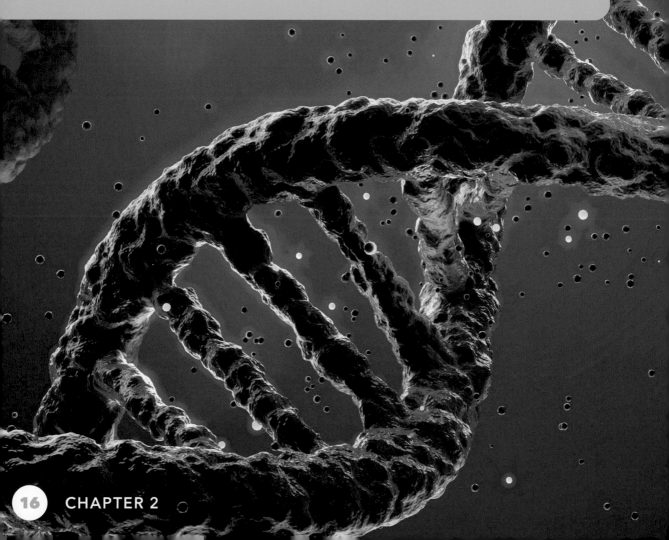

The men told the world about DNA's shape. Knowing DNA's shape changed **genetics**. It helped scientists understand how the genetic code works.

At first, the men left out Rosalind's name. They did not say she helped. No one knew how much work she did.

TAKE A LOOK!

DNA takes the form of a double helix. What does that mean? Take a look!

A double helix looks like a twisted ladder.

Each "rung" is made up of two paired parts. These parts are called **bases**.

The order of the bases forms the genetic code. The bases are like letters that make up words.

CHAPTER 3

DNA TODAY

Scientists now know a lot about DNA. They can see how living things are related. For example, dogs and wolves look alike. They have similarities. They also have differences. DNA shows what those are.

dog

wolf

Things in our bodies hold DNA. Blood and hair are two. Police use DNA to solve crimes. Doctors study DNA, too. They use it to see if a person might get an illness.

Rosalind died in 1958. She didn't get credit for her work. One of her friends was Anne Sayre. In 1975, Anne wrote a book. It explained how Rosalind helped discover DNA's structure. It took time, but Rosalind finally got credit for her work.

DID YOU KNOW?

More people have written about Rosalind. Buildings are named after her.

ACTIVITIES & TOOLS

MAKE YOUR OWN DNA MODEL

DNA forms a double helix. Make your own double helix and explore the structure of DNA with this fun activity!

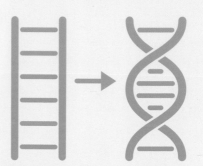

What You Need:
- 4 pipe cleaners
- scissors

① Take two of the pipe cleaners. Cut each pipe cleaner into three equal pieces. You should now have two large pipe cleaners and six smaller pipe cleaners.

② Lay the large pipe cleaners down next to each other.

③ Lay the small pipe cleaners on the large ones as if they were rungs on a ladder. Twist the ends of the small pieces onto the larger pieces.

④ Carefully twist the ladder shape so that each large pipe cleaner forms a helix. Together they form a double helix.

GLOSSARY

bases: Chemicals found in genetic molecules like DNA.

carbon: A kind of matter; coal and charcoal are mostly carbon.

chemistry: The study of matter, what it is made of, and how different kinds of matter act together.

college: A place that teaches higher learning beyond high school.

DNA: A molecule that carries a human's or animal's genes.

efficiently: Working well, quickly, and without waste.

filter: To go through a device to clean a gas or liquid.

genetic code: Information in genes that tells living things how to grow and act.

genetics: The study of how genes are passed from parents to children.

helix: A shape like a wire twirled in circles; a shape similar to a slinky.

molecules: The smallest bits of one kind of matter that still act like themselves.

structure: How something is arranged, organized, or put together.

World War II: A war in which the United States, Australia, France, Great Britain, the Soviet Union, and other nations defeated Germany, Italy, and Japan.

X-rays: Invisible and powerful beams of light that can pass through solid objects.

INDEX

TO LEARN MORE

Finding more information is as easy as 1, 2, 3.

1 Go to www.factsurfer.com

2 Enter "RosalindFranklin" into the search box.

3 Choose your book to see a list of websites.

FACT SURFER